GUINEA PI[G]
PLAN FOR
BEGINNERS

A COMPLETE GUIDE TO WHAT YOUR GUINEA PIG CAN EAT

SAURAV

Copyright 2020 by Guineapig101.Com
All Rights Reserved

This document is geared towards providing exact and reliable information in regards to the topic and issue covered.

The publication is sold with the idea that the publisher is not required to render accounting, officially permitted, or otherwise, qualified services. If advice is necessary, legal or professional, a practiced individual in the profession be ordered.

From a Declaration of Principles which was accepted and approved equally by a Committee of the American Bar Association and a Committee of Publishers and Associations.

In no way is it legal to reproduce, duplicate, or transmit any part of this document in either electronic means or in printed format.

Recording of this publication is strictly prohibited and any storage of this document is not allowed unless with written permission from the publisher. **All rights reserved.**

The information provided herein is stated to be truthful and consistent, in that any liability, in terms of inattention or otherwise, by any usage or abuse of any policies, processes, or directions contained within is the solitary and utter responsibility of the recipient reader.

Under no circumstances will any legal responsibility or blame be held against the publisher for any reparation, damages, or monetary loss due to the information herein, either directly or indirectly.

Respective authors own all copyrights not held by the publisher.

The information herein is offered for informational purposes solely and is universal as so. The presentation of the information is without a contract or any type of guarantee assurance.

Disclaimer

I as an author have made every effort to ensure that the information in this book was correct and updated at the time of release.

The author and publisher do not assume and hereby disclaim any liability to any party for any loss, damage, or disruption caused by errors or omissions, whether such errors or omissions result from negligence, accident, or any other cause.

The authors and publishers advise readers to take full responsibility for the safety of their pets.

The book is intended to help all the beginners and kids to understand the basics of a well-balanced guinea pig diet. However, This book is not intended as a substitute for the medical advice of veterinarians.

Some guinea pigs might have a different need for the food depending upon their medical condition, breed, and current diet.

The reader should regularly consult a veterinarian in matters relating to the health of his/her pet and particularly with respect to any symptoms that may require diagnosis or medical attention.

The author of this book is neither a veterinarian nor a professional guinea pig breeder. He has shared what he has learned from experience and exposure in the last decade or so living with his guinea pigs.

Please consult a vet immediately if your guinea pig is in any kind of trouble or shows any unusual behavior.

Acknowledgment

Thank you for choosing this book! We sincerely hope that this book will be helpful to you in many ways.

In this book, we have tried to provide you with all the information you need to provide a well-balanced diet for your guinea pigs.

The book is well-formatted in an easy to read manner so that even your kids can learn from the book.

All the information presented in the book is shared from the personal experience of the author, and all the data is collected from verified and trusted sources only.

We understand that no guide can be fully complete. That's exactly why our main aim was to create a basic guide to understand the basic dietary need of your guinea pigs.

The author has also shared a few diet plans at the end which has worked for him for several years now.

However, we strongly encourage you to learn more about your guinea pigs from credible sources, talk to other guinea pig owners and pay a visit to the veterinarian in case of any emergency or medical-related conditions.

Table of Contents

Introduction 1
Guinea Pig Diet 3
A Guide For Beginners 3
Vitamin C For Guinea Pigs 5
Calcium In Your Guinea Pig's Diet 11
Hay For Guinea Pigs 23
Vegetable For Your Guinea Pigs 38
Pellets For Your Guinea Pigs 50
Treats For Your Guinea Pigs 55
Water For Your Guinea Pigs 60
Bad Food For Our Guinea Pigs 73
Food To Avoid 73
A Well-Balanced Diet Plan For Guinea Pigs 77

Introduction

If you are a new guinea pig owner, or you have just got guinea pigs as a family pet just like me then you definitely are wondering how you can provide them with excellent care.

The first and foremost thing most new owners struggle with is the diet of their guinea pigs. Yes, diet is extremely important as the health of your guinea pigs is very much dependent upon a good and balanced diet.

Even though guinea pigs are considered a low maintenance pet, understanding their diet can be a challenge for many owners as they struggle to create a diet plan for their guinea pigs.

Thus, I decided to create a wonderful resource for you and your kids so that you can understand all aspects of their diet and provide them with a healthy and happy life.

For your convenience, the book is divided into several chapters where we understand various aspects and parts of their diet.

At the end of the book, I have also created a well-balanced diet plan for your guinea pigs depending upon the availability of fresh food(vegetables & fruits) in the area.

So, as a whole, you get FOUR EXCLUSIVE DIET-PLAN for your guinea pigs which you can follow through during Spring, Summer, Fall & Winter.

The diet plan is made in such a way that it creates the right balance of essential nutrients in their diet but with an option to replace any of the food with what's available at your disposal.

I can assure you that by the end, you will have all the knowledge and information that you need to provide a well-balanced diet for your guinea pigs.

I wish you have a pleasant experience and this book helps you in providing the right care your guinea pig needs for leading a long and healthy life.

GUINEA PIG DIET
A GUIDE FOR BEGINNERS

Understanding what you can feed to your guinea pigs and what you should avoid altogether can be a challenge.

Whenever we get these small little animals home for the first time we have a lot of questions in our mind. One of the major concerns is regarding the diet of our guinea pigs.

However, if you invest some time in understanding the dietary and nutrients needs of your guinea pigs then it can be a cakewalk for you all.

Any new Guinea pig owner can get overwhelmed by the contradictory information and facts lying out there so I decided to put everything that I have researched and found working for me into a single guide for you all.

A Perfect well-balanced guinea pig diet usually consists of Hay, Vegetables, Fruits and Fresh and Clean water.

Now let us see the proper proportion of the same:

- Hay:- 80% of their diet.
- Fresh Vegetable and herbs:- 10-15% of their daily diet.
- Pellet:-5-10% of their diet
- Fresh and Clean Water:-100-300ml at least.
- Occasional- Treats in a small amount.

As every human being has a different taste and preferences, I believe the same is true with Guinea pigs. No single guinea pig is the same.

For instance, Some guinea pigs love cucumber and bell peppers while others love tomatoes and cilantro.

Thus, it can be a little challenging to understand the preference of your guinea pigs and create a balanced diet for them.

However, I am determined to provide you with all the important information so that you can design a diet as per your guinea pig's need and preference.

While looking to create a well-balanced diet for your guinea pigs we must understand and keep a few things in our mind:

- Make sure you have provided an unlimited amount of hay to your guinea pigs.
- Guinea pigs need fresh vegetables daily for Vitamin C and other minerals.
- We must keep the calcium content in their diet to a certain level as a high calcium diet can lead to health issues like sludge and bladder stones.
- Avoid too much sugar and fat in their diet as it is bad for their health as well.

So, with those basics out of the way let us now learn more about Vitamin C and Calcium in your guinea pig's diet.

VITAMIN C FOR GUINEA PIGS

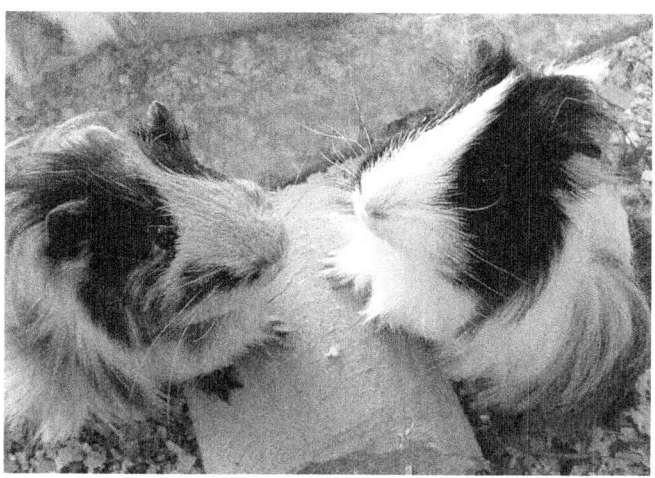

Vitamin C is an essential component of a guinea pig's diet. Due to the lack of ability to synthesize their own Vitamin C, guinea pigs need a supplement of Vitamin C in their food. Thus providing a diet rich in Vitamin C is very crucial for our guinea pigs.

An average guinea pig requires around 10-30mg of Vitamin C daily for every pound of body weight.

A guinea pig who is ill or currently suffering from a deficit of Vitamin C will need around 50mg of Vitamin C every day or as directed by a Veterinarian.

As the requirement of Vitamin C varies depending upon the growth rate, age, and many other factors, **it is always a great idea to be on the higher end(30-50mg).**

Unlike calcium, any extra vitamin c will be excreted by guinea pigs through urine. So, it is wise to provide extra Vitamin C to ill guinea pigs.

Importance of Vitamin C in guinea pig's diet

Vitamin C is essential for the healthy growth of our guinea pigs. It is a crucial nutrient as it helps in the formation of collagen. Collagen is vital for maintaining blood vessel integrity, bone formation, etc.

It also helps in repairing tissue of all parts of the body. Thus, it is an essential vitamin for our guinea pigs.

A lack of Vitamin C in your guinea pig's diet also makes their immune system weak and they are more prone to diseases like scurvy in the long run. Thus, make sure you provide enough Vitamin C to your guinea pigs.

What happens if a guinea pig doesn't get vitamin C?

Guinea pigs who don't get enough Vitamin C in their diet are likely to suffer from various diseases, including abnormal growth, Lack of immunity, and Scurvy.

There are a lot of symptoms of lack of Vitamin C in guinea pigs. We need to look at them carefully and visit a vet if we find any of those symptoms in our guinea pigs.

So, let's have a look at signs of lack of Vitamin C in guinea pigs:

- Rough hair coat or patches in the coat.
- Mouth and lips sore
- Weak and lethargic movement
- Losing weight and improper appetite
- Swollen or bleeding joints
- Small wounds bleed extensively and don't recover fast.
- Diarrhea

If you notice any of these symptoms, then it is recommended to visit the vet and get your guinea pigs examined thoroughly.

Dealing with a lack of Vitamin C in guinea pigs

If your guinea pig shows any symptoms of Vitamin C deficiency, you must first make **an appointment with your vet.**

Your vet will be able to diagnose your guinea pig and check what can be the right treatment for the same.

If the vet confirms that the symptoms your guinea pig is showing are due to lack of Vitamin C then they might ask you to supplement the diet with Vitamin C, fortified food along with some other medical supplement for the same.

Consider adding some Vitamin C rich vegetables and fruits in your guinea pig's diet. Feeding an excess of Vitamin C rich diet will not hurt during this stage.

If your guinea pig is suffering severely due to lack of Vitamin C, then they might be reluctant to eat Vitamin-rich food or even treat. In that case, you must use liquid Vitamin C and use a syringe to feed the same to your guinea pigs. You can also use critical care by some popular brands to supplement their needs.

You can ask your vet for the recommended dose of Vitamin C and administer it for a couple of weeks until you see some signs of recovery.

If even syringe feeding is not working, then you might need to visit the vet regularly to get the Vitamin C supplement injected to your guinea pigs.

Recovery Stage

Once the treatment has begun, your guinea pig must start looking better within a week or so.

Inspect your guinea pigs carefully to see if the symptoms are going away and if they are becoming more active.

If your guinea pig doesn't show any sign of recovery, notify your vet so that he can adjust the dosage of vitamin C accordingly. Once you find your guinea pig is recovering its time to move towards external wounds.

If your guinea pig is suffering from severe scurvy, then you will find some scabbed skin or bleeding wounds.

It's now time to clean the injury regularly and ask your vet for some external medication if necessary.

In most cases, the wound will heal itself once Vitamin C's needs are fulfilled. If you find your guinea pig is suffering a lot and is in a lot of pain, getting a painkiller prescribed for it might be a great choice.

Speak to your vet about the dosage and get one for your guinea pig if necessary.

What can I give my guinea pig for vitamin C?

We need to give our guinea pigs a variety of diets to meet the daily need of Vitamin C in their body.

Although the staple diet for guinea pigs is Hay itself, it doesn't hold much Vitamins C in it. So, a wide range of leafy vegetables, fruits, and pellets are added in their diet to make it balanced.

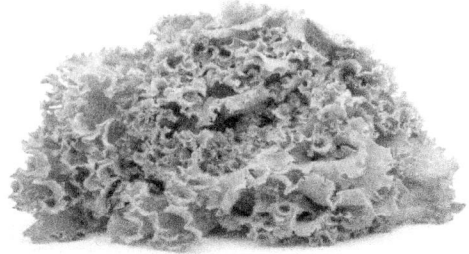

There is a wide range of leafy vegetables and pellets fortified with Vitamin C, which can be a great source of the same.

Alternatively, there are a lot of other supplement medications available, which you can use if your guinea pig is suffering from Vitamin C deficiency.

There is lots of food that we can give to our guinea pigs to fulfill their need for Vitamin C.

Let us check out the list of food which we can provide to our guinea pigs that can fulfill their Vitamin C needs.

Kale	Parsley	Spinach	Cilantro	Bell pepper
Chicory	Dandelion greens	Turnip greens	Romaine lettuce	Brussel sprouts
Watercress	Apple	Apricots	Oranges	Papaya
Strawberries	Kiwi	Guava	Pineapple	Honeydew

Please note that fruits cannot be served regularly as they contain a lot of sugar in them.

Do guinea pigs need vitamin C tablets?

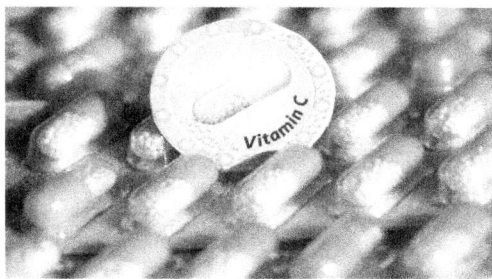

No, it is not recommended to feed Vitamin C tablets to your guinea pigs until and unless they are suffering from Vitamin C deficiency.

In general, if you feed a proper diet with fruits, vegetables and pellets rich in Vitamin c your guinea pigs are unlikely to suffer from lack of Vitamin C.

However, if your guinea pigs are suffering from lack of Vitamin C you can supplement it by giving them a quarter of a chewable Vitamin C tablet.

In general, Vitamin C tablets come in 100mg sizes. So, a quarter feeding will almost provide 25 mg Vitamin C to your guinea pigs.

Calcium in your guinea pig's diet

Calcium is an essential nutrient required by everyone, and guinea pigs are no exception. Guinea pigs need calcium for the formation of bones, teeth, and other vital organs of the body.

However, most guinea pig owners end up feeding excess calcium to their guinea pigs, which increases the risk of health issues, including bladder stones and sludge.

So now we shall discuss how you can reduce calcium in your guinea pig's diet!

Guinea pigs with stone & sludge problems eat the same diet proportion, but with controlled portion sizes.

Replacing the hay with good quality high fiber timothy hay, Low calcium vegetables, and providing enough hydration is the best way to reduce calcium intake of your guinea pigs.

The primary goal of reducing calcium in your guinea pig's diet is not to eliminate it altogether.

It is meant to control the excess calcium that goes into their body and leaves via the urinary tract.

In the long run, the calcium starts getting deposited in the bladder resulting in the formation of bladder stones in guinea pigs.

Is calcium good for guinea pigs?

Yes, calcium is an essential mineral for our guinea pigs. It is crucial for the formation of healthy bones and teeth in your guinea pigs.

The deficiency of calcium in your guinea pig's diet can result in Hypocalcemia. It is a condition when the calcium level in the blood of your guinea pigs goes below the minimum level.

Hypocalcemia can be extremely dangerous as your guinea pigs might pass away due to this condition without showing any signs of severe health issues.

Thus, make sure you don't reduce calcium to an extreme level in your guinea pig's diet.

Low calcium diet for guinea pigs

If your guinea pig is diagnosed with bladder stone or sludge, your vet will recommend serving a low calcium diet to your guinea pigs.

Now, what the vet means here is not to eliminate everything that has calcium in it from your guinea pig's diet.

Instead, control the proportion & type of food being served to reduce the overall intake of calcium in your guinea pig.

Calcium is present in all kinds of food. Right from the hay, vegetables, plants, herbs, fruits, pellets, and even water, everything has some amount of calcium in it.

Thus, it is impossible to eliminate calcium altogether. We must aim to create a well-balanced low calcium diet for our guinea pigs.

However, to create a low calcium diet for our guinea pigs, we first need to understand how much calcium is required by our guinea pigs & how do guinea pigs absorb calcium from their food.

How much calcium do guinea pigs need?

According to a study conducted by The National Academy of Science, average guinea pigs need 8 grams of calcium/Kg of their body weight.

This means if the weight of your guinea pig is one kg, then they will need 8 grams(8000mg) of calcium every day.

Weight Of Your Guinea Pigs	Daily Calcium Requirement
900 Grams	7200mg (7.2 grams)
1000 Grams	8000mg (8 grams)
1100 Grams	8800mg (8.8 grams)
1200 Grams	9600mg (9.6 grams)

You can use the above table as a reference and understand the calcium requirement of your guinea pigs as per their body weight.

Do remember that Young guinea pigs (age up to 16 weeks) need more calcium in their diet as their body grows at a rapid pace.

However, once your guinea pigs mature, they require less calcium in their diet.

If your guinea pigs have been diagnosed with bladder sludge or stones, then chances are, they are consuming more calcium than what is recommended for them.

You might need to monitor everything that goes into their diet to understand the calcium intake and regulate it accordingly.

Your vet may recommend the amount of calcium you need to serve to your guinea pigs.

Even if they don't, you can use the above data as a baseline and serve the food accordingly to your guinea pigs.

How does a guinea pig absorb calcium?

Guinea pigs have an unusual way of absorbing calcium from food.

When a guinea pig eats any food, the food passes through the esophagus and reaches the intestines.

Here the pipes break the food into small particles absorbing the nutrients present in it.

In most mammals, the calcium and other vital nutrients absorption are managed by the parathyroid hormone (PTH).

However, in guinea pigs, it is not well-regulated.

According to a study, Guinea pigs absorb 50% more calcium from food than what a regular human being does.

Thus, their body ends up absorbing most calcium from the food. As a result, the amount of calcium intake is directly proportional to the calcium present in their diet.

Effects of high calcium diet in guinea pigs?

When guinea pigs absorb more calcium than their body needs, the excess calcium is excreted in the form of urine from the urinary tract.

In the long run, the excess calcium gets deposited in the bladder, forming calculi.

In guinea pigs, solid calcification can be formed in the bladder, urinary tract, etc. Thick calcium sludge can also get accumulated in the bladder that can lead to other urinary tract issues as well.

According to a study, It is quite reasonable to detect some mild calcium in your guinea pig's urine once in a while.

However, in some guinea pigs, the extra calcium can bind together to form thick sludge or stones that can be difficult to pass out.

It might even require surgical removal in some cases, as it is harrowing for your guinea pigs.

Reducing calcium intake of your guinea pigs

Reducing calcium intake of your guinea pigs is really simple and straightforward.

You just need to monitor what goes into your guinea pig's diet and at what quantity to create a healthy balance.

Chances are you are feeding excess calcium to your guinea pigs in some form.

Now what you need to do is reduce the amount of calcium by substituting some high calcium food items with a lower calcium substitute.

Also, there is one major factor to remember while looking at the calcium content of the food. i.e., Dry foods like hay & pellets have high concentrations of calcium as compared to fresh food like vegetables & fruits. Thus 5% calcium in hay is way more than 5% calcium in vegetables & fruits.

Hay and Fresh Grass

Hay is the staple portion of a guinea pig's diet, and you need to keep it that way. 80% of your guinea pig's diet should consist of hay as it helps in maintaining their digestive system, helps them in maintaining their teeth, etc.

While hay does contain some calcium content in it, you still want to keep it as a significant portion of your guinea pig's diet.

Types Of Hay/Grass	Calcium Content
Timothy Hay	0.4-0.6%
Orchard Hay	0.33%
Meadow Hay	0.6%
Alfalfa Hay	1.3%
Oats Hay	0.4%
Fresh Grass	0.35%
Watercress	4%

As you can see the best hay for your guinea pigs shall either be timothy hay or orchard hay as it contains the least amount of calcium in it.

Avoid alfalfa hay at all costs as it contains over 1.3% of the calcium in it.

One of the significant challenges in hay is most of the guinea pig owners end up buying bulk hay or cheap quality hay.

Now the quality of those hays is not bad, but what the company does is mix some alfalfa hay in those timothy and orchard hays to bring the cost of the product down.

As a result, you end up feeding excess calcium to your guinea pigs.

So, if your guinea pig is suffering from problems of bladder stone or sludge, I would strongly recommend starting feeding good quality timothy hay or orchard hay only.

Fresh grass

Alternatively, you can also start replacing a small portion of their hay with homegrown grass.

Please don't throw in a bunch of fresh grass from your lawn, as it may contain some harmful chemicals that can harm your guinea pigs.

However, if you have time, you can grow in some fresh grass in containers and start replacing a small portion of your guinea pig's diet with that fresh grass.

Fresh grass contains far less concentration of calcium due to high water content and is an excellent replacement for hay in such a scenario.

Pellets

Pellets are another dry food that contains a decent amount of calcium in it.

Controlling the amount of calcium in pellets is complicated, and there are only two ways you can achieve it:

- Reduce the consumption of pellets and replace them with some additional vegetables.
- Serve low calcium pellets to your guinea pigs.

Many new guinea pig owners often make a mistake of choosing the wrong type of pellet.

While selecting the pellet, you must lookout for the calcium content in it and the base of the pellet as well.

Avoid pellets that have more than 0.6% calcium content in it. Also, make sure the pellet is timothy based and not alfalfa based.

However, make sure your guinea pigs eat a lot of vegetables rich in Vitamin C else your guinea pigs might suffer from another major health issue, also known as Scurvy.

Low calcium vegetables for guinea pigs

Vegetables are also an integral part of your guinea pig's diet. A guinea pig needs a cup(125 grams) of fresh veggies daily.

You can drastically reduce the calcium intake of your guinea pigs by substituting some vegetables in and out from their regular diet.

For example, the calcium content of carrot(100 grams) is 33 mg, whereas calcium content in Kale (100 grams) is 254 mg.

However, the portion size matters too. A slice of carrot has more mass than a small leaf of Kale.

Vegetables contain a decent amount of water in it. Thus, the concentration of calcium in the vegetable is quite less as compared to pellets.

"For example, 25grams of pellets contains approximately 200mg of calcium in it. While 25 grams of kale only contains around 65 grams of calcium in it."

Here are some popular low calcium vegetables for your guinea pigs. We have also mentioned an approximate amount of calcium content per serving according to our guinea pig's dietary needs.

Vegetables	Approximate Calcium(25grams Serving)
Carrots	8.25
Tomatoes	2.5
Bell peppers	2.5
Red Leaf Lettuce	8.25
Green Leaf Lettuce	9
Cilantro	16.75
Cucumber	3.5
Zucchini	5.25
Cabbage	10
Celery	10
Broccoli	11.75

Thus, fresh vegetables can be an excellent replacement for pellets in your guinea pig's diet.

Adding some extra fresh vegetables won't add much of excess calcium in your guinea pig's diet while adding some extra pellets can make a ton of difference in the same.

Water consumption of your guinea pigs

Water consumption has a direct impact on bladder stone or sludge issues. There are mainly two ways of how water consumption can affect it:

- Different types of water contain different levels of calcium in it.
- Adequate water consumption can dilute the urine thus it also dilutes sludge buildup in the bladder.

Calcium content in water

Drinking water has a varying amount of calcium in it depending upon the type of water and the area you live in.

Hard water has eight times more calcium than soft water.

While soft water usually contains 15mg calcium/liter, hard water contains over 120mg calcium/liter.

Thus, make sure you serve only soft water to your guinea pigs. If soft water is unavailable in your area, you can also get some bottled water for your guinea pigs.

You can also increase the water intake by serving more fresh food and decreasing the quantities of pellets from your guinea pig's diet.

Fresh pasture grass is also an excellent replacement for hay that can help increase the water intake of your guinea pigs.

How can drinking more water prevent bladder stones in guinea pigs?

Increasing the amount of water intake of your guinea pig is an excellent method to dilute the urine and prevent the formation of thick sludge in your guinea pig's bladder.

A guinea pig can drink anywhere between a 100-300ml of water every day.

The consumption of water is dependent upon the type of food, weather, living environment, kind of water available, etc.

Now there is nothing much you can do to increase the water consumption of your guinea pigs directly. However, there are a few tips you can follow to increase it by a little bit:

- Add more than one source of water in your guinea pigs enclosure.
- Provide more watery vegetables and fruits.
- Replace their dry food(pellets) with some extra green veggies.
- Refill fresh water in the bottles at least 2-3 times a day.
- Make sure the water you are serving is of room temperature.
- Avoid any additives like Vitamin C drops as guinea pigs can smell and taste it, and thus they will drink less water.

How do you prevent bladder stones in guinea pigs?

There are a variety of factors that can lead to the formation of bladder stones in guinea pigs. Here are few ninja tips you must remember to prevent bladder stones in your guinea pigs:

- Ensure your guinea pigs get the right type of hay as per their need and age. While young guinea pigs(up to 16 weeks age) need alfalfa-based hay, mature guinea pigs need Timothy-based hay to meet their dietary requirement.
- Good quality timothy based pellets with less than 0.6% calcium content should only be fed to your guinea pigs.

- Include a mix of low calcium vegetables with high calcium vegetables to create a well-balanced diet for your guinea pigs. Never serve high calcium vegetables on consecutive days.
- Increasing the amount of Vitamin C in the diet of your guinea pigs also helps prevent diseases.
- Replace pellets with fresh veggies if your guinea pigs show any sign of sludge in the urine.
- You can also replace a small portion of hay(10-15%) with fresh green pasture. Green and fresh foods have a low concentration of calcium in it. However, make sure the grass is organic and free of chemicals.
- Encourage your guinea pigs to drink more water. Adequate water consumption can dilute the urine and prevent the formation of sludge in the bladder.
- Always make sure you serve soft water with low calcium content in it. Hard water contains eight times more calcium than soft water. Thus, avoid it altogether.
- It is also seen that potty training your guinea pigs often increases the frequency of urine, and thus, it reduces the chances of formation of sludge.

HAY FOR GUINEA PIGS

You might have heard people saying that "Hay is a staple part of a guinea pig's diet & guinea pig's diet should contain at least 80% hay in it." but there are still a lot of questions that can boggle a new guinea pig owner's mind.

In this section of the book, I have tried going through some of the basics of hay, which hay you should buy, how much hay should you buy for your guinea pigs and much more. So, let's begin!

Why do guinea pigs need hay?

Guinea pigs get essential fiber and nutrients from the hay, which is crucial for the proper functioning of their body.

Lack of hay in their diet can cause fiber deficiency, which further leads to poor digestion and abnormal growth in them.

Thus, hay is an essential part of your guinea pig's diet.

Why the quality of hay matter?

The quality of hay is directly proportional to the health and well-being of your guinea pigs.

What most new owners make a mistake with this as they chase after the remaining 20% i.e providing their guinea pigs with the right type of vegetable & pellets and its serving size, etc.

However, while they are busy improving that 20% they neglect the most essential part(80%) of their guinea pig's diet. i.e hay.

Yes providing your guinea pigs with the right type of pellets and good vegetables is important but providing them with good quality hay is the most important thing.

Studies claim that providing the right type & good quality of hay can improve your guinea pigs lifespan by several folds. It can also reduce the chances of diseases which in turn is beneficial in the long run.

What most people here think is that whether you get a big bale of hay or a pack of hay from the store it is the same thing.

" Hay is hay" right? Absolutely wrong! So, does that mean your guinea pigs will not enjoy the hay from a bale than from a bag? No, even that is not true.

It is all about quality at the end. Like we human beings nowadays prefer organic fresh vegetables and food over the regular type right? Why? Because we know it is of good quality which will keep us healthy. The same goes for your guinea pigs as well.

Some people also get the cheapest quality hay possible to save on the monthly expense, but here is what you should know! *Most cheap quality hay is mixed with different types of poor feeds and fillers like alfalfa, etc to get the cost down.*

Yes, it may save you some money($) in the short term but in the long run, you will end up spending more in a vet clinic trying to fix a health issue that could have been avoided in the first place if you had brought good quality hay for your guinea pigs.

I don't want to say that only packaged hay is good for your guinea pigs and you should get that only.

What I want you to understand is it is completely fine even if you get a bale of hay from the farmer in your area. But make sure what you are getting is good for your guinea pigs.

Just don't buy a bale from anyone because he/she is offering you a great deal for the same. Just make sure you are serving the right type as well as good quality hay to your guinea pigs.

The best type of hay for guinea pigs?

Timothy hay is the best type of feed available for your guinea pig. It has the perfect balance of fiber, protein, and calcium, which is required by our guinea pigs.

Although there is a wide variety of hay available right from Alfalfa, Meadow to Oats and Bermuda, still timothy hay is the first choice among most guinea pig owners.

Types of hay:

There is a wide variety of hay available in the market. However, not all types of hay are equally good for our guinea pigs.

A lack of proper guidance and understanding can make the choices difficult and even wrong in some cases.

Thus, it is really crucial that you understand what types of hay are good for your guinea pigs and why.

So, let us begin by having a look at six common types of hay available in the market.

Timothy hay:

Timothy hay is the most widely used hay among all guinea pig owners. This hay is readily available, has a pleasant aroma and tastes really well, which makes it the absolute favorite of all guinea pigs.

However, if you dive in a little deeper you will learn that even timothy hay is further divided into three types depending upon the seasonal cut. i.e.

- 1st cut Timothy hay
- 2nd cut Timothy hay
- 3rd cut Timothy hay

Now let us have a closer look at what is the difference in these different seasonal cuts of hay.

1st Cut Timothy Hay	High fiber, Low Fat & Protein	Ideal for guinea pigs with dental issues & Gastro-intestinal issues
2nd Cut Timothy Hay	The ideal ratio of all Nutrients	Perfect for healthy guinea pigs
3rd Cut Timothy Hay	Low fiber, High Fat & Protein	Ideal for sick guinea pigs who need to gain weight or have some chewing problem or mouth pain.

You need to choose the right variant depending upon your guinea pig's health and physical conditions. In most cases, we serve 2nd cut Timothy hay to our guinea pigs.

However, if your guinea pigs have some dental issues or they need to gain some weight then you might have to go with the other two variants.

Please note: You should not go with 3rd cut timothy hay unless it is recommended by a professional expert or veterinarian. This hay contains low fiber and high fat that can lead to health issues in guinea pigs if fed regularly.

Alfalfa Hay:

Alfalfa hay contains a high concentrate of Fiber, Protein, and Fat, which should not be a part of the daily diet of your guinea pigs.

Feeding your guinea pigs with alfalfa hay regularly can lead to weight gain and obesity, which is not suitable for their health.

In fact, Alfalfa hay also contains a high amount of calcium in it, which is terrible for your guinea pig's health.

Too much calcium in their diet can lead to the formation of bladder stones, diarrhea, and other health issues.

Although there is an exception to the rule if your guinea pig is nursing or very young.

As these would need more amounts of nutrients in that phase, so adding some alfalfa hay in their diet turns out to be helpful.

But make sure you don't make it their daily diet as the calorie intake would be much higher than required in that case.

If your guinea pig is suffering from some health issues and needs to gain some weight, then your vet may recommend adding some alfalfa hay into their diet. You can add the recommended amount during that phase as well.

Alternatively adding a small quantity of alfalfa hay once in a while can spice things up for any adult guinea pigs although the amount must be restricted so that they don't suffer any consequence due to it.

Meadow Hay:

Meadow hay consists of Soft stemmed grasses, clovers, leaves, flowers and seed heads of other edible plants like dandelions, daisies, etc.

Basically, anything that is in the meadow while harvesting ends up in the bag for your guinea pigs. Green, long grass strands are the distinct characteristic of this hay.

Meadow hay is softer than Timothy hay, which is pleasant for some guinea pigs to munch on.

While some guinea pigs love the added flowers and stem in their food, the other's hate it, it depends upon their personal choice.

Meadow hay is also less dusty as compared to other feeds, which makes it a great option, especially if you are allergic to Timothy hay.

The long strands of grasses in this hay are rich in fiber and other nutrients which is essential for guinea pigs.

It not only helps in maintaining good dental health but also aids in digestion, which is a bonus.

If you are choosing Meadow hay, then go for long green strands one as they are fresh and nutritious.

Bermuda Hay:

Bermuda hay is high-quality hay that is rarely used as a feed for guinea pigs.

Although it is used as a feed for some other larger animals, it is an excellent source of fiber as it contains 32% crude fiber in it.

It includes some moderate amount of Fat and Proteins, which makes it a great choice, although the price and availability is the crucial factor which makes it a rare choice among guinea pig owners.

Bermuda hay also lacks the proper balance of nutrients and hence is not the best choice for your guinea pigs.

Oats Hay:

Oats hay is yet another unconventional choice among guinea pig owners. These hays have a long stem with oats attached at the end of it. They are usually yellowish in color and definitely not so pleasant for the eyes.

It contains a high amount of fiber protein and fat, which is suitable for adult guinea pigs which need extra nutrients.

Also if your guinea pig doesn't like 1st cut Timothy hay, then you might go for Oats hay, but it is not ideal for other guinea pigs.

Although you can add it once in a while in a small quantity to spice things up, it should definitely not be a part of their daily diet.

Orchard hay:

Orchard hay is an excellent choice for guinea pig owners suffering from allergies. This hay has the perfect balance of Fiber, Fats, and Protein required by our guinea pigs.

Orchard hay has a broader leaf as compared to Timothy hay, but the texture is really soft, which makes it really easy for guinea pigs to chew.

It also makes a great bedding choice due to its smooth texture. If you are going for orchard hay get a new bag and make sure it is green and mold-free.

You can replace Timothy hay with orchard hay but make sure you only buy the best quality one for your guinea pigs.

Why is hay important for guinea pigs?

Good quality hay provides your guinea pigs with essential nutrients needed for proper growth in your guinea pigs.

1. **Source of nutrients:** Hay is a vital source of essential nutrients like Fiber, Fat, and Protein. These nutrients are crucial for proper growth in guinea pigs. They also provide enough calories which are required by the guinea pigs daily.

2. **Helps in maintaining digestive health:** Hay is rich in fiber, which is required for maintaining their digestive health. Guinea pigs have sensitive digestive organs, and if we don't provide them with the proper diet, they may suffer from diarrhea and other diseases.

3. **Helps in wearing down of teeth:** Hay not only helps in maintaining good digestive health but also aids in wearing down the teeth of our guinea pigs. Hay contains silica that naturally wears down your guinea pig's molar teeth. As you might already know guinea pigs have ever-growing teeth that need the constant wearing down. If your guinea pigs don't get enough hay, then they will develop dental issues, including overgrown teeth, which can be fatal in some instances.

4. **Natural Bedding Material:** Hay also acts as a natural bedding material for your guinea pigs. Good quality hay is absorbent and soft, which can add an extra layer in your existing bedding.

Guinea pigs do love to burrow and to have a pile of hay for them to play with really helps with it. It also helps in insulation during the winter, thus keeping your guinea pig a little warm.

How much hay do you need for a guinea pig?

Provided that your guinea pigs have FREE ACCESS to hay, an adult guinea pig can consume anywhere between 6-8 pounds(3-4 kg) of hay every month.

If you have a young guinea pig, you can expect them to go through 5-6 pounds(2-3 kg) every month.

There are a few factors, including the quality of hay, the health of guinea pigs, and their overall diet, which can impact the consumption of hay.

You can feed an unlimited amount of Timothy hay to your guinea pig. However, if you are feeding some other type of hay in the mix like oats hay or alfalfa hay, then you must restrict the quantity.

In general, your guinea pig must have access to hay and water at all times. They constantly chew on hay to keep their digestive system well balanced. Remember to provide fresh hay and water every day so that they remain healthy and happy.

How much hay do guinea pigs eat per day?

An adult guinea pig can eat anywhere between 90-100 grams of hay every day. It will be a wise decision to provide fresh hay at least twice daily.

You can create 1-2 piles around their cage to forage and eat. Also, make sure you always have extra hay available for your guinea pigs.

Sometimes guinea pigs go through their hay pretty quickly and in such a scenario, you always want to provide them with some extra pile so they don't run out of hay anytime soon.

Can guinea pigs survive without hay?

No, Guinea pigs cannot survive without hay for long. A healthy guinea pig can live up to 24 without hay, the next 24 hours is going to be very difficult for them, and they may not even survive after that.

Hay is a vital source of fiber and other essential nutrients without which they may suffer from various digestive issues and other diseases.

These diseases can get worse in no time and can be life-threatening as well provided you don't feed them with the right diet.

Can you feed a guinea pig only hay?

No, you cannot feed only hay to your guinea pigs. Although 80% of their diet must be hay, it still lacks one major nutrient i.e., Vitamin C in it.

A guinea pig cannot synthesize their Vitamin C; thus they need a supplement in the form of Fruits, Vegetables, and Pellets in their diet.

Feeding your guinea pig with only hay might lead to diseases like scurvy in the long run.

"A well-balanced daily intake of a guinea pig must contain an unlimited amount of hay, 1 cup of vegetables, 1/8 cup of pellets and some occasional fruits and treats."

Why is my guinea pig not eating hay?

There can be a lot of reasons due to which your guinea pigs might not be eating an adequate amount of hay. Let us have a look at some of the most common cause:

They don't have easy access to hay

Many people often get tempted to use some unique style hay racks, which definitely look great but don't serve the purpose all the time.

Some of the hay racks hinder the accessibility of hay to your guinea pigs. Some hay racks like hay balls often carry a risk of getting your guinea pigs head stuck into it.

Thus, using something different might look unique but can discourage your guinea pigs from eating their food.

The hay is of poor quality

Hay is the most significant part of your guinea pig's diet. It provides your guinea pigs with the most vital nutrients, including fiber, which they need in abundance.

Providing cheap quality thin vacuum-packed hay to your guinea pigs is not the best idea.

If you care about the good health of your guinea pigs and want them to live a long life, then provide then learn a little bit about good quality hay for your guinea pigs and offer them one if you can.

There are a few things you need to check to ensure the hay is of good quality for your guinea pigs:

- Dry, first cutting hay
- Mixed texture; neither too thin nor too coarse
- Green, fresh free from any molds
- Even better if it contains seed heads

Your guinea pig is having some health issues

Guinea pigs are prone to dental issues, which can hinder their ability to consume food effectively.

As we know, guinea pigs have an ever-growing tooth which needs to be continuously worn down to keep it in check.

Sometimes their molar teeth overgrow and form a bridge shape over their tongue, which makes eating food extremely difficult for them. Since we can't tell the shape of molars just by looking at our guinea pigs, it is challenging to determine.

Often, this is the reason why many guinea pigs starve to death because we are unable to determine why our guinea pig is not eating enough food.

It is recommended to seek expert veterinarian advice ASAP if your guinea pig is not eating food properly.

The proportion of their diet is incorrect

We often get carried away looking at our cute guinea pigs when they wheek and ask for food.

As a result, we end up feeding them a lot of goodies in their diet. Many people also get tempted to throw in some extra veggies into their cage, although it might affect their health negatively in the short term, it does have its effect in the long run.

Guinea pigs don't care about 80% hay rule, or in lay man's words, they don't have control over their diet.

If you end up feeding them more goodies like carrots and bell peppers, they will be more than happy to munch on it.

However, we should only feed them hay in unlimited quantities and serve vegetables in small amounts.

Can guinea pigs be allergic to hay?

No, guinea pigs are not allergic to hay. However, sometimes hay comes with a lot of dust in it, and that can cause an allergic reaction in guinea pigs.

If your guinea pigs show some apparent signs like sneezing, watery eyes, etc. just after serving hay to them, then you should be suspicious towards the hay.

However, hay consists of 80% of your guinea pig's diet, and there is no way we can eliminate hay from our guinea pig's diet.

The dust in the hay causes most of the allergic reaction to hay, and that is what we must focus our attention on.

Different types of hay come with a different level of moisture and from different yields.

These are the primary factors that affect the amount of dust hay produces when being handled.

How to deal with hay allergy in guinea pigs?

If you have recently got a new bag of hay and you notice specific allergies symptoms in your guinea pigs, then there are a few ways to deal with it without wasting the hay.

- Pull out a pile of hay and put it in a storage container. Now you can carry the box to somewhere like your sink and fluff up the hay a little bit to get rid of extra dust. Now place the hay back into the cage.
- You can use a hay feeder pouch. It helps by containing all the hay, and thus less dust gets spread around your guinea pigs.
- Lightly mist the hay with a spray bottle to keep the dust level low.
- Lastly, you might need to switch to a different brand or quality of hay.
- You can also try orchard hay as they tend to be less dusty as compared to timothy hay. Orchard hay has similar nutritional value as timothy hay.

Please note: Any change you make might take a few days to reflect on your guinea pig's health and behavior.

How to store hay for guinea pigs?

Storing the hay for your guinea pigs can be pretty straightforward. There are three major things we need to keep our hay safe from. i.e., Rodents, Sunlight, and Moisture.

The best practice is to use a resealable bag which is free from moisture and place it in a cool, dry area.

Just make sure that any other rodents like mice etc. cannot reach the hay. The second most important thing is to ensure that the feed is stored away from direct sunlight.

Direct sunlight can make the hay extra dry, and it will lose some nutrients in the process.

The third and most important factor is to make sure there is no moisture in the hay or the bag where you keep the hay.

Hay can get moldy pretty quickly in the presence of moisture. So, make sure the hay is stored dry and free from any moisture.

Also, avoid feeding the hay if it gets moldy as it can cause various diseases in your guinea pigs.

How long does hay last for?

If you can store the hay correctly, then your hay will last for a long time(over a year) on your shelves.

However, it is not recommended to store feed for that long and serve it to your guinea pigs.

Studies have found that hay stored in a shelf loses its nutritional value over time.

Thus, it is recommended to buy and use hay in small packs as and when needed.

I prefer to buy a bag that lasts me for a month and get another one in advance just for safety so that I don't run out of hay anytime soon.

Can guinea pigs eat grass instead of hay?

No, guinea pigs cannot eat grass instead of hay. You can definitely feed some grass along with side hay sometimes, but it definitely is not a substitute to hay.

Hay contains a lot of fiber and other nutrients that grass cannot provide. Also, most grass is treated with pesticides and other chemicals that are lethal for guinea pigs.

Vegetable for your guinea pigs

Are vegetables essential for guinea pigs?

Yes, Vegetables are really a key aspect in their diet that cannot be neglected. Keeping a mix of vegetables into the diet is essential to provide their bodies with all the necessary nutrients.

Unlike other animals, Guinea pigs cannot produce Vitamin C and some other vital nutrients on their own.

They need to be served the right quantity and mix of vegetables to live a healthy life. Vegetables also provide them with hydration in their bodies.

However, the key to a balanced diet for your guinea pig is to serve variety but in moderation.

How much vegetables do guinea pigs need every day?

Guinea pigs need a cup of fresh veggies on a daily basis. You need to provide a mix of 4-5 types of vegetables to create a well-balanced diet for your guinea pigs.

You can mix two leafy vegetables with some vegetables high in Vitamin C(staples) like bell peppers, cilantro, etc. and follow up with 1-2 other vegetables to create a well-balanced diet.

List of vegetables for your guinea pigs

Guinea pigs need a cup of fresh vegetables daily. However, not all vegetables are suitable for feeding your guinea pigs on a regular basis.

Here is a list of vegetables divided into three major groups based on the suggested servings.

Almost Daily

Bell peppers(Green & Yellow)	Cilantro(10-15 sprigs)	Green Leaf Lettuce	Red leaf Lettuce
Romaine Lettuce(alternate days)	Banana Leaves	Wheatgrass	Corn Husk

2-3 times a week

Carrots	Tomatoes	Clover	Broccoli leaves
Cabbage (Red)	Cauliflower leaves	Parsley	Mint
Bell pepper(Red & Orange)	Green beans	Chicory	Collard Greens
Cucumber	Zucchini	Radicchio	Belgian Endive

1-2 times a week

Green cabbage	Spinach	Basil	Broccoli
Cauliflower	Mustard green	Thyme	Asparagus
Corn	Peas	Eggplant	Moringa
Bok Choy	Bean sprout	Brussel Sprout	Arugula
Beet greens	Kale	Okra	Parsnip
Chards	Turnip	Watercress	Radishes

How To Prepare Vegetables For Guinea Pigs?

Preparing vegetables for your guinea pigs can be confusing for some of us. Here are simple steps you can follow for the same:

- Get fresh vegetables for your guinea pig.
- Next, you need to wash the vegetables properly as it may have traces of chemicals attached to it. Cleaning it properly is vital to ensure the good health of our guinea pigs.
- You also need to chop the vegetables into small pieces and serve the recommended serving of a cup(130-140 grams) by mixing at least 4-5 different vegetables together.
- Prepare a cup of fresh veggies and serve it to your guinea pigs. You can also serve it 1/2 cup in the morning and remaining at night to ensure they get a good meal throughout the day. (P.S. It also helps reduce their noises at night)
- Lastly, you need to remove any uneaten fruits or vegetables from the cage to avoid fly and rats infestation in the cage.

Are Cooked Vegetables good for a Guinea pig?

No, Guinea pigs cannot eat cooked vegetables at all. Cooked food is terrible for our guinea pig's health as it can set their digestive system off-balanced due to other ingredients being added in the process of preparing the food.

Cooking the food also kills some crucial nutrients that are needed by our guinea pigs.

Thus, make sure you only serve fresh and raw vegetables to your guinea pigs.

Can guinea pigs eat frozen vegetables?

Yes, guinea pigs can eat frozen vegetables but only after it is being thawed and brought to room temperature before serving.

Serving frozen vegetables to your guinea pigs can off-set their digestive system that can be terrible for their health. *Thus, make sure you don't serve cold food directly from your fridge.*

Can guinea pigs eat canned vegetables?

No, guinea pigs cannot eat canned vegetables at all.

Studies claim that canning vegetables need extra additive color, preservatives, sugar or salt, and various other ingredients that are bad for our guinea pig's health.

Thus, make sure you only serve fresh vegetables to your guinea pigs.

Can guinea pigs go without vegetables?

Ideally, you never want to leave your guinea pigs without vegetables on any day.

Vegetables are an integral part of your guinea pigs diet as it provides your guinea pigs with much-needed Vitamins and minerals.

However, if your guinea pigs don't want to eat their veggies, and in such cases, you can supplement their diet with high-quality pellets for a short amount of time.

But in the long-term, you must ensure that your guinea pig's diet gets enough share of veggies so that they can stay healthy and live a long and comfortable life.

Why won't my guinea pig eat vegetables?

If you bought your guinea pig from a pet store or other unreliable sources, then there are high chances your guinea pig hasn't even tasted any veggies yet.

So, getting adjusted to a new food might need some patience at your end as well. Apart from that, Too much pellet based diet or some health issues like dental problems could be a culprit as well.

A guinea pig needs to eat at least 10% of their body weight in the form of veggies(approx a cup). These vegetables help provide essential Vitamin C and other Vitamins that our guinea pigs cannot produce on their own.

I can totally understand how mind-boggling it could be when your guinea pigs don't eat their veggies or have suddenly stopped eating.

But you should not worry at all, today we shall learn how you tackle this problem with a practical approach which is recommended by most guinea pig experts(breeders & fellow keepers).

The first and foremost thing we must do is to understand why your guinea pigs are not eating their veggies. This can help you find a possible solution to feed them.

There can be a lot of reason due to which your guinea pigs might not be eating their veggies.

Today we will check out some of the most common reasons which our experts have sighted:

Check your guinea pig's history

One of the most common mistakes that new guinea pig owners make is buying their first guinea pig from a pet store or other unreliable sources.

Now you might be wondering what is wrong with those places? The fact is these stores often feed only pellets and low-quality food items to the guinea pigs, which is the reason your guinea pigs are reluctant to eat those veggies when you first get them.

If possible, ask the people who were looking after your guinea pigs earlier about their diet so that you know what your guinea pigs are used to eating. This will ensure you have a starting point to go ahead with.

Let your guinea pigs settle down a little bit

When we get a new guinea pig home, they might need some time to adjust to the change in the environment.

While some guinea pigs get comfortable quite quickly, others take more time for the same. So, if you have just brought your guinea pig, then it is quite natural for them not to eat properly or avoid a certain kind of food.

Guinea pigs often get frightened easily, so it can also be one possible reason why your guinea pigs are not eating enough food.

Check out their diet proportion

Would you eat your favorite food when your stomach is full? No, right most of us won't eat it. The same might go for guinea pigs as well.

Check what you are feeding to your guinea pigs. A guinea pig's diet must contain an unlimited amount of good quality hay, 1/8 cup of pellets, and fresh veggies daily.

If you are feeding more pellets and treats to your guinea pigs, then it is quite possible that they are already full, and they won't eat the veggies you offer to them.

Most guinea pig owners make a mistake of feeding too many treats to their guinea pigs.

Just because your guinea pigs ask and wheeks for the treats you shouldn't be feeding it in excess quantity as it can disbalance their diet completely.

The veggie you are trying to feed is not the right one for them

Just like human beings, guinea pigs can be picky about what they eat. While some guinea pigs like having a particular type of veggie, the other might hate it completely.

There is a possibility that the kind of vegetables you are offering to your guinea pigs is not what they like to eat.

As you never know what type of diet was being provided to your guinea pigs before you got them, there is a possibility they eat only a particular kind of food.

I had seen a guinea pig eating only one specific brand of the pellet when I first got her. You might need to be patient enough for them to gradually switch over to the right kind of diet you want to offer to them.

They have some health issues

Health issues can be another significant cause behind your guinea pig, not eating their veggies or food.

One of the most common health issues which can hinder their diet is their overgrown molar teeth. It is quite tough even for an experienced owner to tell if their guinea pigs have an overgrown tooth.

Often the molar teeth overgrow and block the passage above their tongue, which can hinder the ability to chew and swallow the food in guinea pigs.

How do I get my guinea pig to eat vegetables?

By now, you must have already understood that there can be a lot of factors that can hinder the proper diet of your guinea pigs.

I know how much stress it can be if your guinea pigs don't eat the veggies daily.

But you needn't worry at all; Today, I am going to share a few tips up my sleeves, which can help you out in feeding veggies to your guinea pigs.

Have patience and introduce one veggie at a time

If you have got a new guinea pig and they are not eating fresh vegetables at all, then it can be a little stressful for you, but I would suggest you stay calm.

In fact, this can be happening due to either of these two reasons.

The first one being your guinea pigs were never fed vegetables in the past, so it is completely new stuff for them, and the second one being they need some time to adjust in the new environment.

In either case, you need to be very patient. Don't add further stress to your guinea pigs by offering a variety of new food.

In fact, the right choice would be to start with one or two vegetables, preferably lettuce and a carrot.

Once your guinea pigs get accustomed to these, you can begin adding variety in their diet.

It is quite possible that your guinea pigs won't eat the veggies for the first few days.

You need to be patient and persistent and keep offering fresh vegetables daily so that they can get the hang of it.

Every guinea pig have their own taste and preference

As we had discussed earlier, it is quite possible that your guinea pig doesn't like a particular type of veggies that you are offering.

You can try offering different vegetables every few weeks so that you can learn about what kind of veggies your guinea pigs like.

There are over 60 different types of veggies that you can feed to your guinea pigs. You can try feeding different combinations and find what your guinea pigs like and what they don't.

If they start eating a particular one, you can keep that in the diet and replace the other one to find out more. Over time your guinea pigs will start eating different types of veggies with no problem at all.

Get a knowledgeable company

Getting a good cage mate who loves too much on their veggies could be an excellent motivation for your new guinea pigs.

When your new guinea pigs watch other guinea pigs eating their vegetables, they feel more comfortable in munching those and in the process, will learn to eat the veggies.

If you don't have a cage mate, then you can be one and try chewing a few bits alongside their cage so that your guinea pigs give it a shot as well. It is just like a mother teaching their babies to try new food.

Start with a non-watery vegetable

If you are introducing vegetables for the first time in your guinea pig's diet, then it would be a wise decision to start with some non-watery veggies.

Carrots, Lettuce, Bell peppers, etc. could be a great choice, to begin with. You can also serve Coriander or Cilantro in a small quantity if they didn't like anything else.

Once they get used to these veggies, then moving on to some watery vegetables like Zucchini, Cucumber, etc. will be a great move to make.

Please note: Not all guinea pigs will eat a variety of veggies. Some like to stick with a particular one. If you have once such a guinea pig, then changing their diet very slowly is the right choice to make. Introduce one new veggie at a time replacing some old ones, and over time, you can teach your guinea pigs to munch on all different types of vegetables.

Always ensure you feed them fresh veggies only

Whenever you are feeding vegetables to your guinea pigs, you need to ensure you feed only fresh veggies to them.

Guinea pigs can get sick if they are supplied with stale veggies. Even when you are trying to make your guinea pigs accustomed to vegetables, it is a wise move to offer veggies in small quantities 2-3 times a day.

Changing the veggies after every few hours will ensure that the veggies remain fresh and will also encourage your guinea pigs to nibble on the same.

Visit a vet for a checkup

Dental problems in guinea pigs can often hinder the diet of your guinea pigs. Visiting a vet would be great if you feel that your guinea pigs are not eating enough food.

Sometimes, getting their molars trimmed often does the trick, while other times, a minor surgery might be needed. In either case, getting advice from a professional expert can be life-saving for your guinea pigs.

Pellets for Your Guinea Pigs

Although hay is a staple diet for any Guinea pig occasionally a guinea pig must also be served with Pellets specially designed for them.

When served in the right quantity alongside Hay and fresh vegetables it will help in providing them with balanced nutrients that their body needs.

Do guinea pigs need pellets?

Yes, guinea pigs need pellets especially if they don't enjoy vegetables rich in Vitamin C.

Most pellets made for guinea pigs have a decent amount of Vitamin C in it that helps supplement their need for vitamins and minerals.

Thus, it is important to introduce a small serving of pellets into your guinea pig's diet.

What kind of pellets should I feed my guinea pig?

The choice of pellets for your guinea pig is entirely dependent on their age. If your guinea pig is a young one(less than twelve months of age), then you should feed them pellets containing alfalfa in it.

On the flip side, mature guinea pigs over twelve months of age should only eat pellets with Timothy in it.

You should also feed any nursing or pregnant guinea pigs with pellets based on alfalfa as it contains necessary calcium for their body.

What are guinea pig pellets made of?

Different brands producing guinea pigs use a different mix of ingredients, So we must make sure to have a look at them while selecting the pellets for your guinea pig.

Pellets with high-quality ingredients provide more nutrition, which is essential for your guinea pigs.

You must look for at least 20% fiber and 12-15% protein in the pellets we are buying for our guinea pigs. Added Vitamin C is yet another bonus as it is also essential for guinea pigs.

Try to stay away from anything that contains seeds, nuts, oil, rice bran, ground corn, and other similar ingredients.

Avoid artificial chemicals

We must also stay clear from all the artificial chemicals, food colors, and other added additives in the pellets.

Some of the primary ingredients to look for are:- sucrose and corn syrup. Also, chemical additives like sodium nitrite, nitrate, or metabisulfite are a significant threat to your guinea pigs.

So, it is best to stay clear on all those additives while choosing pellets for your guinea pigs.

Timothy Vs Alfalfa

Deciding on Timothy and alfalfa-based ingredients in the pellets is yet another crucial decision to make. While alfalfa-based pellets are going to be rich in calcium and fat due to the presence of alfalfa, the Timothy based pellets contain a balance of all nutrients.

So, if you are looking for pellets for young or nursing guinea pigs, then you should go ahead with pellets based on alfalfa while for matured guinea pigs timothy based pellets are going to be a suitable choice.

You must also consider that serving an alfalfa-based pellet to mature guinea pig can lead to the formation of bladder stones.

As their body doesn't need the extra calcium, it binds in their bladder, forming the stones which are very painful for them.

While the stones can be removed with surgery, it definitely is not a pleasant experience for your guinea pigs.

How often do you feed guinea pigs pellets?

As per the recommendation, we must feed 6 grams of dry food for every 100 grams of weight. It merely means anywhere between 1/8th cup to 1/4 cup of pellets would be a great point to start with.

But can we overfeed pellets to our guinea pigs? **No, you definitely can't even if you provide guinea pigs with an unlimited amount of hay and pellets they won't overeat and fall sick. However, if you find them munching on pellets all the time then you might need to restrict the serving.**

However, it is still essential to limit the serving size. Why? It is best to serve fresh pellets every day to our guinea pigs. Pellets in a bowl might get dirt and other unwanted things accumulated around it.

Also, guinea pigs like to toss their food around or even pee and poop in their food bowls sometimes so you don't want to leave it like that. Do you?

Are rabbit and guinea pig pellets the same?

No, guinea pigs cannot eat the pellets meant for rabbits. However, the rabbits might eat the pellets made for our guinea pigs.

Guinea pigs pellets are specifically designed keeping in mind the nutritional need and type of food for our guinea pigs. Thus, we must only serve guinea pig food pellets to our guinea pigs.

Tips to introduce pellets into your guinea pig's diet

Introducing pellets to your guinea pigs is really simple. You can take a good quality food bowl and put around 1/8 cups of pellets in it and place it in your guinea pigs cage.

Watch from a distance if they smell it out, or try some bits and pieces of it or not. If you find they just smelled and left the food, you can try mixing it with some treats and try again so that they can eat it and get the taste of it.

Do it slowly, and you will definitely end up introducing it in their daily diet

If you are already serving another brand of pellets to your guinea pigs and want to introduce a new one you should try mixing a small quantity of new one with the old one and serve the same to your guinea pigs.

If your guinea pig likes the taste, you can gradually increase the quantity and fully replace it in due course of time.

How long do guinea pig pellets last?

If you store the pellets properly a bag of pellets won't go bad for 6 months to a year. However, in most cases, it won't last that long anyway.

If you feed pellets to your guinea pigs regularly, then a 5-pound bag for two guinea pigs would typically last for a month or so.

In general, I like to grab a big bag as pellets don't go bad over time, and a big bag is way cheaper in the long run.

It might not be right for you if you are getting alfalfa one, but for the timothy pellets getting the big bag is the best choice you can make.

How to store guinea pig pellets?

Here are a few tips to keep pellets fresh for long:

- Store it away from direct sunlight.
- Use an airtight bag or container to keep it safe from molds.
- Never use any wet spoon or hand while fetching the pellets.
- Make sure the location where the pellets are kept is dark and dry.
- Some people prefer to store it in the freezer however it's not needed at all.

TREATS FOR YOUR GUINEA PIGS

No guinea pig owner can resist feeding some small treats to their guinea pigs every now and then. In fact, many owners use these treats as positive reinforcement while training their guinea pigs.

But are all the treats available in the market suitable for your guinea pigs? What are some of the best guinea pig treats you can buy?

Treats for guinea pigs?

When it comes to treats for guinea pigs, then there are lots of options out there. Your furry friend won't care much until and unless the food tastes good to them.

But bear in mind, every guinea pig has its own taste preference, while some guinea pigs like a particular food while others don't. You shall need to do some trials and errors to find out what type of food keeps your guinea pigs happy.

Fruits

Fruits are a typical treat for guinea pigs. They are high in sugar so we cannot feed it regularly. While we can definitely serve a small quantity now and then.

It is recommended to help fresh fruits one to two times a week as it also contains some beneficial vitamins in them.

Some of the great choices of fruits for guinea pigs are:- Apples, Oranges, Kiwi, Watermelon & Strawberries.

Commercial Treats

There are a lot of commercial treats available in the market which we can feed to our guinea pigs.

While the commercial treats can be on a dearer side when compared to fresh fruits, they do add a little diversity in the diet we usually offer.

What treats are bad for guinea pigs?

Yes, Guinea pigs can eat a lot of fruits and vegetables just like us, but we cannot feed our guinea pigs with treats we eat usually.

Treats like Cookies, Chocolates, Milk-based items or any other items we eat are not at all suitable for our guinea pigs.

Guinea pigs can only eat treats prepared explicitly for them. It can either be one that is homemade or commercially prepared but should be made keeping their diet in mind.

How many treats should we serve to our guinea pigs?

In general, treats only form 10% of their total diets. As we know, treats contain some high sugar ingredients **which we cannot feed more than once a week.**

In general, I prefer to serve a small serving of treats to my guinea pigs. The amount offered depends upon treat to treat.

For fruits, a little slice or so is preferred, and for other commercial treats, I will suggest one or two small pieces depending upon the size should be enough.

Can guinea pigs have dog treats?

No, dog treats are definitely not recommended for your guinea pigs. Many people who have dogs, as well as a guinea pig, think that they can share the same treats but the fact is they can't.

The treats made for dogs contain some cereals, sugar, etc. in high amounts, which is not so favorable for your guinea pigs.

Can guinea pigs have yogurt treats?

Yes, guinea pigs can eat yogurt treats but only in moderation. Many people would say that yogurt is bad for their digestive system as they are lactose intolerant.

The saying might hold true for general yogurt we eat but when it is added in small quantities in preparation of their treat it might not hurt them much.

I have tried a few famous brands like Kaytee and Oxbow yogurt-based treats and they were awesome. My guinea pigs loved them.

What fruits can we serve to our guinea pigs?

Here is a list of fruits that you can serve to your guinea pigs. Please note that these fruits should never be made a regular part of their diet. These should be served sparsely as a treat only.

Apple	Banana	Blackberries	Blueberries	Breadfruit
Cantaloupe	Carambola	Cherries	Clementines	Cranberries
Elderberries	Gooseberries	Grapefruits	Grapes	Guava
Honeydew melon	Java-Plum	Kiwi	Kumquat	Lemon
Longan	Lychee	Mandarin	Mango	Mulberries
Nectarines	Olives	Orange	Papaya	Passion fruit
Peaches	Pears	Persimmon	Pineapple	Plums
Pomelo	Raspberries	Strawberries	Tangerine	Watermelon

WATER FOR YOUR GUINEA PIGS

Water is an essential part of the diet for a Guinea pig. We must always ensure that our Guinea pigs have access to Clean and Fresh drinking water at all times.

How much water does a guinea pig need?

Guinea pigs can consume anywhere between 50ml to over 300ml of water every day. They require fresh and clean water all the time.

Although, The amount of water they need does vary for every individual guinea pig. You should always ensure that your guinea pig has fresh water all the time.

How much water do guinea pigs drink every day?

The consumption of water also depends upon their body weight. **Usually, 20% of their weight is the amount of water they consume daily.**

Both extremes can be just fine as it all depends on one guinea pig to another. The consumption of water by them depends on a lot of factors like:

- Weather conditions
- Indoor heating/cooling.
- Diet etc.

So, it is totally fine even if your Guinea pig is drinking 60-70 ml of water or 300ml of water until and unless that is their regular consumption.

But, if you see any significant change in water consumption, then you must immediately try to know the cause of the same and fix it.

Can guinea pigs drink tap water?

I often see people getting confused with whether they should give their guinea pig distilled water, tap water, or any sort of special water made for the rodent.

What I have learned is if you give your guinea pig the water you can drink then its totally fine for them. **You should never give your guinea pig distilled water.** Simple filtered tap water would just be great for them.

Always ensure that the water is free from any sort of chemicals and contamination. It is also essential to provide them with water at room temperature.

Can guinea pigs drink cold water?

You could give them somewhat cold water in scorching summer but try to stick with room temperature on any usual day. You should not provide them with warm water as they refuse to drink that at all.

Your guinea pig must NEVER be fed Alcohol, Aerated water, or anything similar to it. Serving those may lead to fatal health issues or in the worse case, a Life threat for them.

Should I add any supplements to the water for my Guinea pigs?

There are a ton of medicines and vitamin supplements that can be added to their water. However, do not add any sort of vitamin additives or minerals in the water because in most cases, they will try to avoid drinking much of it.

Avoiding water for long may lead to dehydration in them in the long run. Adding additives to water also makes them a home for algae, which is a bad thing for your guinea pigs.

Also adding any sort of medication to water is a bad idea because you cannot control the intake of water.

Also, most of the medications are really bad in smell and taste so your guinea pig will not even bother going near to it.

The guinea pig has double the number of taste buds as compared to humans. So, you cannot fool them that easily.

How should I provide water to my Guinea pig?

Provide your guinea pig with water in a way they are comfortable with, and they can have access to it at all times.

There are many different ways to provide them with fresh water, but the choice of it will be dependent upon your guinea pig preference. You need to do some trials and see which system they prefer the most.

Can guinea pigs drink water from Bottles?

The plastic and glass bottles are widely being used all around the world for providing water to the guinea pig.

Unfortunately, there is no leak-proof and problem-free bottle available in the world just yet so we must depend upon it in most cases.

Both the glass and plastic bottle is clipped from outside the cage with the pipe like nozzle reaching in from which Guinea pigs can sip the water. Although this is better than bowls as they are less prone to contamination and refilling is quite easy too.

It is preferred to get a glass bottle instead of a plastic one because those are less prone to the algae issue.

The room temperature will vastly not impact the water if it's in good glass bottles. Also, the glass bottle has a larger nozzle size, which makes it more comfortable for a guinea pig to use. But at the same time, plastic bottles are way cheaper than a glass bottle.

Although widely used these types of bottles come with a significant disadvantage. Firstly, It is really tough to create a vacuum so that the bottle doesn't drip or leak.

Many people try to fill the bottle till the end so that it doesn't drip, but that is not the right way and in cold regions water may freeze and burst the bottles in some cases.

Secondly, In this type of bottle Guinea pigs must use their tongue to hit the ball in the nozzle so that the water comes out, which makes it difficult to drink much water at once.

Also, they usually drink water after having food, so the pellets or food in their mouth gets stuck in the nozzle and can very often choke it.

Bonus tip

Always have an extra set of bottles because you will need to replace them every 10-12 months as they get worn out over time. It is also healthy to keep changing plastic dishes to prevent health issues.

Can guinea pigs drink water from Sippy Bottles?

Sippy bottles are excellent in comparison to standard bottles for any guinea pig. It is much easier for them to drink water from this type of bottle as they simply need to raise the gib at the nozzle, and a continuous stream of water will start flowing in.

Using sippy bottles will also lead to more water consumption as they need not struggle to do so as in the case of standard bottles. If given a choice any guinea pig will lean towards this bottle more.

The build quality of these bottles is excellent as it uses much thicker plastic, making it less prone to algae. This bottle does not work on the principle of vacuum, thus it is less likely to clog.

Although these bottles also have a disadvantage, Sometimes they continue to drip water, and so a drip dish is required below it so it doesn't create a mess.

Can guinea pigs drink water from a bowl?

Bowls are the easiest way to supply water to the guinea pigs. Always remember to use heavy ceramic bowls so that they cannot tip them over.

Usually, guinea pigs tend to place their front paws in the bowl while drinking, which can lead to tip over if the dish is unsuitable for them.

Younger guinea pigs who haven't yet learned to drink from bottles must be provided with water in a bowl so that they do not suffer.

Also, the bowl makes it easier for them to drink as they can just get the water by dipping the head into it. But for some reason, Guinea pig does not like to drink water from Bowls.

Bowls also have a significant disadvantage that the water is more prone to. The feces and food particles often get dropped in it and make water contaminated.

So it is best to avoid it unless and until necessary. Sometimes when the guinea pig is sick and is unable to drink water from the bottle then they can be given a bowl to drink with.

How can I teach my Guinea pig to drink from the bottle?

In young ages, Guinea pigs tend to drink water from bowls rather than bottles. It is always good to encourage them to drink from bottles as it is more hygienic.

Do not worry, they will learn to feed on bottles by watching their parents and elders do the same. You can encourage this mostly by placing a small ceramic container just below the tip of the bottle.

Although you may need to change the water 3-4 times a day because a lot of feces and dirt will get accumulated into it.

After some time you can place some bits of cucumber on the nozzles or anything else they like just to make them try it. Usually, within a few weeks, your Guinea pigs will get used to it and will start drinking water from it.

Alternatively, you can take the bottle in hand and put some treat in the nozzle and bring it near its mouth to get them started.

Do not force this upon your Guinea pig as this may lead to even further worse situations in time to come. You will also stress them out a lot by doing so, which is not what we want to do.

We want positive reinforcement and not the negative one. Please fill fresh and clean water every day in the bottle even if not in use. Not changing the water daily will result in algae formation.

How to place water bottles in Guinea pigs cage?

Although this might look like a fundamental question, it's actually an important one because if your Guinea pig needs to stretch out to reach the water, they will be negatively enforced to drink much.

Also having it too low will make them duck in for it again not something you want. Having the water bottle at the correct height is pretty essential and must be learned by beginners while starting out.

Although in general keeping the nozzle at the height of 1-2 inches works excellent, it is vital that you try other possibilities too. As not all guinea pigs are the same.

I would recommend putting 2-3 bottles at a different height and see what works the best for you. Also having multiple bottles helps because if one gets blocked, the other one can be used.

How should I clean the water bottle or bowl of my Guinea pig?

Here you have mostly two methods you can go with. Let's have a look at both of them:

Firstly, Get a commercial cleaning kit that every pet store supplies and use the same to rinse off your bottles and bowls.

It's quite simple; Just pour the cleaning agent, take the brush and scrub it off from inside and outside and then rinse it off and it's done.

Secondly, The more hygienic and budget-friendly way is to take a bit of uncooked rice and some water in the bottle.

Now, Place a finger in the lid/opening to close it off and shake vigorously. Then empty your dish, and it's spotless!

Always rinse the nozzle too as it contains the most amount of dirt and leftovers. Use a cotton bud by dampening it to clear the ball nozzle.

Always use a baby bottle disinfectant to clean the bottle once in a week or so. It's imperative to provide your Guinea pigs with fresh and clean water.

How can I monitor the amount of water my guinea pigs are drinking?

The most natural way to do so is by using a bottle to feed them the water. In most situations, your pet water consumption will remain consistent.

Although weather change and temperature may bring a small change gradually. If you refill the container daily on a schedule, you will be able to monitor the water consumption of your Guinea pig.

It is crucial you follow this quite closely as any significant change in water consumption is the starting sign of sickness in a Guinea pig.

If you find your Guinea pig has a substantial change in water consumption, then it's best to give a visit to the vet.

Is my guinea pig drinking too much water?

The ideal consumption of water by a guinea pig is usually 20% of its body weight. Now, this may depend from pig to pig.

Some drink around 50-60 ml a day while some drink 200-300 ml. It is quite okay if the consumption is not unusual.

But sometimes there are notable changes in water consumption. If your guinea pig is drinking too much water it may be because of the following reasons:-

- If you change the diet of your guinea pig, it may trigger some unusual behavior. Sometimes a change in diet can lead to more water consumption than earlier.
- If you serve more veggies rich in the water earlier, then a change in that can cause more water intake. The same way more hay consumption increases water intake.
- Change in temperature can also sometimes trigger some change. If there is a change in temperature, then it might be the reason for more water consumption. As heat increases the need for water usually goes up too.
- Sometimes dental issues, Bladder stones, urinary tract infections, etc. may also lead to more consumption of water.
- Diabetes is also a reason that increases water intake. You need to do the blood test for detecting the same in your guinea pigs.
- Major health issues like kidney failure and digestive disorder can also lead to an increase in water intake.

If there is a notable increase in water consumption of your guinea pig and you are unable to figure out the reason, then it's best to take them to a vet soon.

You could wait for a day or two and keep a close eye on any other health issue symptoms. But the best would be to take them to the vet as soon as possible.

Is my Guinea pig Drinking too little water?

Sometimes we feel that our pet might be drinking too little water. But that can be due to many reasons.

Sometimes it's a regular change whereas sometimes a serious one. Here are the few things to notice if your guinea pig is drinking less water than usual:-

- If there is a change in the diet mostly to more veggies and fruits, then it can lead to less water consumption.
- In a cold environment, water consumption usually goes down.
- The taste of water is changed either due to some chemicals like chlorine etc. or due to added supplement by you, which is a common issue that leads to less water consumption.
- Sometimes diseases like Mouth infection, Dental overgrowth, Pneumonia, or respiratory problems can also lead to less water consumption.

Again, I would suggest taking them to the vet if you are unable to understand the cause. In the meantime, provide them with water-rich veggies like cucumber, celery will fulfill their hydration needs.

What are the symptoms of Dehydration In Guinea pigs?

It might be really tough for a beginner to understand if its pig is dehydrated or not. Unlike other pets, guinea pigs are really good at hiding their illness.

So, you must keep a close eye on these signs to detect if something is wrong or not.

- Keep a close eye on their pee(stool) color and smell. Generally, the stool color changes dark orange or brown and smells strong when they are dehydrated.
- You must look closely in their mouth gums. If the gums are dry then its clear sign of dehydration
- Check if your Guinea pig is not as active as usual and have been not interacting much then this might also be the reason.
- Check whether the poop shape is as usual or not. Checking the poop also helps us in understanding many things. Dry and small dropping are the signs of a dehydrated body.
- Look at their eyes up close. If you see dry eyes, sunken eyes then this may also be the cause of dehydration.

How long can guinea pigs go without water?

A Guinea pig can live up to 8-12 hours without water. But sometimes they are seen living up to 48 hours provided it has enough vegetables to eat.

Most of the water requirement of guinea pigs tend to be fulfilled by fresh veggies. So if you feed them a lot of veggies rich in the water they can live for a day or two without water too.

Although we recommend having access to fresh and clean water all the time. If a guinea pig doesn't have enough water to drink for more than a day, it might lead to dehydration and liver problems in them.

Also eating hay makes them more thirsty, so if only a hay-based diet is served to them with no water, then it may lead to a severe situation.

Should I Buy Filtered or low calcium water for my Guinea pigs?

If you live in an area where there is hard water coming in your tap Maybe, then you must consider giving your Guinea pig filtered water.

Many people Don't realize that most of the calcium in the diet of Guinea pigs come from water and not only pellets and veggies.

Providing your guinea pig with water rich in calcium can lead to diseases like Bladder stones or sludge. You must always test your water before you start serving it to your Guinea pigs.

Some people also tend to buy bottled water for guinea pigs without realizing that unlike said those bottles have high calcium content.

It is best recommended to serve your Guinea pig with filtered water to avoid any possible health issues.

Is adding sugar or honey in the water of my Guinea pig safe?

From what I have learned, sugar is not beneficial to anyone. Some beginners try to put some sugar or honey in the water of Guinea pigs just because they think it will increase the water consumption.

Maybe it can do so but it's absolutely not recommended at all. Introducing sugar or honey to the diet of a Guinea pig is equal to inviting a bunch of health problems with it.

You can alternatively use some treats like cucumber pieces etc. in a water bottle nozzle to do so. Never ever try to use Sugar just to increase the water consumption of your Guinea pigs.

Will my Guinea pig drink more water if I put hay in it?

Putting hay in the water is a bad idea.

Firstly the hay will go moldy when you put it in water or moist.

Secondly, When the guinea pigs try to dip their mouth into the water bowl to eat hay, They may end up with water in their lungs from the nostrils.

This will further lead to health issues like Pneumonia. The best way is to put a lot of dry hay and Feed them a lot of hay.

Eating dry hay will make them thirsty and thus drink more water eventually. You can also feed your Guinea pigs with the right amount of veggies that will also fulfill the need of water in their body.

My Guinea pig is not drinking water at all. What should I do?

Sometimes it is quite natural for a guinea pig not to drink water at all. If you have fed him some good fresh veggies like cucumber etc. which have a high degree of fluids, it will fulfill its water needs.

You may notice whenever their vegetable intake goes up, their fluid needs to go down.

This is quite natural and you should not worry much about such a case. But, If you find some sudden changes in water intake without any change in diet, then you must look deeply.

If your Guinea pig is less active than usual, have its eyes closed more, If it is not responding well and also their diet has changed, then something surely is going wrong. If any of the above symptoms are seen, you must visit your vet as early as possible.

Sometimes if a Guinea pig is not drinking water then it could also be because of these reasons:-

- The water bottle nozzle is clogged up with some uneaten food or any other particles. And they are unable to actually drink from it.
- The water contains more chlorine or some chemical which is causing the issue.
- The bottle is not clean properly, leading to poor water quality thus avoiding the water.

Some quick tips you can try if you see the problem persist:-

- Clean the water bottle properly at least twice a week and change it if necessary.
- Check if the nozzle is blocked and clean it with a soft cotton bud.
- Serve only filtered water that is free from any chemical or additives.
- If you are too worried, serve them more of fluid rich vegetables like cucumber and celery. Eating these veggies will prevent dehydration for some time.
- Rush to a vet as soon as possible in case the problem lasts for more than a day.

BAD FOOD FOR OUR GUINEA PIGS
FOOD TO AVOID

What foods are toxic to guinea pigs?

There is a wide range of food that guinea pigs cannot eat. Right from various human food to fruits and vegetables, there are a lot of things that you need to keep in mind while feeding a guinea pig.

Some of the most common food that is toxic to our guinea pigs includes:

Meat	Milk	Yogurt	Cheese	Cream
Iceberg lettuce	Avocado	Onions	Leeks	Chives
Hot peppers	Dry beans/peas	Sour Krauts	Wild Herbs	Wild Flowers
Shallots	Garlic	Avocado	Lentils	Anything with glue, varnish, dyes, etc.
Nuts & Seeds	Salt	Chocolate	Branches and Stems (except few)	Amaranth Leaves
Bitter melon	Broad beans	Cassava	Soybeans	Fiddlehead
Ginger	Wasabi	Potatoes	Tomatillo	Coconut
Date Fruit	Jackfruit	Olives	Plantain	Prunes
Rhubarb	Mamey Sapote	Soursop	Tamarind	Vanilla Bean
Juices	Sweets	Pickles	Cooked food	Food meant other animals

- Dairy Products: Avoid dairy products like curd, milk, cheese, etc as it can lead to digestive problems in guinea pigs.
- Avocado: Avocado contains a lot of fat in it. It also contains a fatty acid like a chemical called persin, which can be harmful to your guinea pig's digestive system.
- Coconut: Coconut is another fruit that we should not feed to our guinea pigs. It contains a lot of saturated fat that can have a bad impact on their health. Some guinea pigs are also allergic to coconut.
- Alcohol: Alcohol is purely toxic to our guinea pigs. Even a single drop of alcohol can put your guinea pigs in sleep mode forever. Thus, avoid it altogether.
- Chocolate: Chocolate is bad for our guinea pigs as guinea pigs cannot digest it well.
- Seeds(sunflower, etc): Seeds contain a decent amount of fat in it. Thus, avoid it altogether.
- Nuts & dry fruits: Most nuts and dry fruits have some decent amount of sugar and fats in it. Both of these are bad for our guinea pig's health thus it is best to avoid it altogether. They also possess choking hazard in some cases.
- Pickles: Pickles contain vinegar and other preservatives which can cause health problems in guinea pigs

- Cooked food: Cooked food loses essential vitamins and minerals. It also needs the addition of other ingredients like oil, salt, etc. These ingredients are harmful to our guinea pigs. It can also lead to diarrhea and other health issues.

- Fruits and vegetables: Some fruits and vegetables are high in oxalic acids, sugar or some other ingredients that our guinea pigs cannot ingest well. Thus, make sure you avoid it altogether.

- Caffeine: Caffeine in the form of tea or coffee is also bad for our guinea pig's health.

- Salt: Most salt is made by processing and adding some chemicals into it. They also contain an excessive amount of sodium in it. Thus, avoid salt altogether.

- Plantain: It contains a decent amount of sugar in it, thus it should be avoided at all costs.

A Well-Balanced Diet Plan For Guinea Pigs

A well-balanced diet for your guinea pigs includes the following:

- Unlimited amount of hay. (Serve one/two pile twice a day)
- 1 cup(125 grams) of fresh veggies. (A mix of 4-5 different veggies)
- A small serving of pellets. (⅛-⅙ of a cup)
- A small serving of treats whether fruits or commercial treats. (1-2 times a week)
- Fresh and Cool Water

Most people struggle with vegetables the most as it is really difficult to decide what you should be serving to your guinea pigs.

I know it can be tough to think of a well-balanced diet plan for your guinea pigs. We need to create a balance of Vitamin C, Calcium as well as other nutrients to create a good diet plan.

Thus, I decided to give you all a plan I usually follow for my guinea pigs.

You can either use a similar diet plan or modify my current plan and make one suitable for your guinea pig's preference. So, let us have a look at the diet plan:

Vegetable Diet For Spring

Day	Staple(1-2 vegetables)	Leafy Greens(1-2 Vegetables)	Other Vegetables(1-2 vegetables)
Monday	Bell pepper (Green/ Yellow)+ Cilantro(10-15 sprigs)	Red/Green Lettuce+Red Cabbage	Carrots+Broccoli/Cauliflower
Tuesday	Bell pepper (Green/ Yellow)+ Cilantro(10-15 sprigs)	Red/Green Lettuce+Kale or Spinach or Chard	Cherry tomatoes
Wednesday	Bell pepper (Green/ Yellow)+ Cilantro(10-15 sprigs)	Romaine Lettuce+Red Cabbage	Carrots+Broccoli/Cauliflower/Peas
Thursday	Bell pepper (Green/ Yellow)+ Cilantro(10-15 sprigs)	Red/Green Lettuce+Spinach or Collards or Arugula	Cherry tomatoes
Friday	Bell pepper (Green/ Yellow)+ Cilantro(10-15 sprigs)	Romaine Lettuce+Red Cabbage	Carrots+Broccoli/Cauliflower
Saturday	Bell pepper (Green/ Yellow)+ Cilantro(10-15 sprigs)	Red/Green Lettuce+Kale or Spinach or Chard	Cherry tomatoes
Sunday	Bell pepper (Green/ Yellow)+ Cilantro(10-15 sprigs)	Romaine Lettuce+Red Cabbage	Carrots+Broccoli/Cauliflower/Peas

Vegetable Diet For Summer

Day	Staple(1-2 vegetables)	Leafy Greens(1-2 Vegetables)	Other Vegetables(1-2 vegetables)
Monday	Bell pepper (Green/ Yellow)+ Cilantro(10-15 sprigs)	Red/Green Lettuce+Red Cabbage	Carrots+Broccoli/ Cauliflower
Tuesday	Bell pepper (Green/ Yellow)+ Cilantro(10-15 sprigs)	Red/Green Lettuce+Kale or Spinach or Chard	Cherry tomatoes
Wednesday	Bell pepper (Green/ Yellow)+ Cilantro(10-15 sprigs)	Romaine Lettuce+Red Cabbage	Carrots+Broccoli/ Cucumber/Zucchini
Thursday	Bell pepper (Green/ Yellow)+ Cilantro(10-15 sprigs)	Red/Green Lettuce+Spinach or Collards or Arugula	Cherry tomatoes
Friday	Bell pepper (Green/ Yellow)+ Cilantro(10-15 sprigs)	Romaine Lettuce+Red Cabbage	Carrots+Cauliflower/ Cucumber/Zucchini
Saturday	Bell pepper (Green/ Yellow)+ Cilantro(10-15 sprigs)	Red/Green Lettuce+Kale or Spinach or Chard	Cherry tomatoes
Sunday	Bell pepper (Green/ Yellow)+ Cilantro(10-15 sprigs)	Romaine Lettuce+Red Cabbage	Carrots+Broccoli/ Cucumber/Zucchini

Vegetable Diet For Fall

Day	Staple(1-2 vegetables)	Leafy Greens(1-2 Vegetables)	Other Vegetables(1-2 vegetables)
Monday	Bell pepper (Green/ Yellow)+ Cilantro(10-15 sprigs)	Red/Green Lettuce+Red Cabbage	Carrots + Beet greens
Tuesday	Bell pepper (Green/ Yellow)+ Cilantro(10-15 sprigs)	Red/Green Lettuce+Kale or Spinach or Chard	Cherry tomatoes
Wednesday	Bell pepper (Green/ Yellow)+ Cilantro(10-15 sprigs)	Romaine Lettuce+Red Cabbage	Carrots + Cucumber/ Zucchini
Thursday	Bell pepper (Green/ Yellow)+ Cilantro(10-15 sprigs)	Red/Green Lettuce+Spinach or Celery or Brussels Sprouts	Cherry tomatoes + Radishes/ Parsnips
Friday	Bell pepper (Green/ Yellow)+ Cilantro(10-15 sprigs)	Romaine Lettuce+Red Cabbage	Carrots + Cucumber/ Zucchini
Saturday	Bell pepper (Green/ Yellow)+ Cilantro(10-15 sprigs)	Red/Green Lettuce+Kale or Spinach or Chard	Cherry tomatoes
Sunday	Bell pepper (Green/ Yellow)+ Cilantro(10-15 sprigs)	Romaine Lettuce+Red Cabbage	Carrots + Cucumber/ Zucchini

Vegetable Diet For Winter:

Day	Staple(1-2 vegetables)	Leafy Greens(1-2 Vegetables)	Other Vegetables(1-2 vegetables)
Monday	Bell pepper (Green/ Yellow)+ Cilantro(10-15 sprigs)	Red/Green Lettuce+Red Cabbage	Carrots + Beet greens
Tuesday	Bell pepper (Green/ Yellow)+ Cilantro(10-15 sprigs)	Red/Green Lettuce+Kale or Chard	Any Other Vegetable
Wednesday	Bell pepper (Green/ Yellow)+ Cilantro(10-15 sprigs)	Romaine Lettuce+Red Cabbage	Carrots
Thursday	Bell pepper (Green/ Yellow)+ Cilantro(10-15 sprigs)	Red/Green Lettuce + Brussels Sprouts	Cherry tomatoes + Radishes/ Parsnips
Friday	Bell pepper (Green/ Yellow)+ Cilantro(10-15 sprigs)	Romaine Lettuce+Red Cabbage	Carrots
Saturday	Bell pepper (Green/ Yellow)+ Cilantro(10-15 sprigs)	Red/Green Lettuce+Kale or Chard	Any Other Vegetable
Sunday	Bell pepper (Green/ Yellow)+ Cilantro(10-15 sprigs)	Romaine Lettuce+Red Cabbage	Carrots

Please note: You can replace one leafy green with any other kind of leafy vegetables available. Also, the other vegetables can be replaced with what's available. You can choose any vegetables from the list we had discussed earlier in the vegetable section of our book.

The serving sizes of vegetables are as follows:

- The standard serving of leafy vegetables is 1-2 small leaves.
- Bell peppers should be served in small slices. (Approx ⅙ to ⅛ of a whole)
- Cilantro should be served in a small quantity. (10-15 sprigs)
- Other vegetables can be served in a small slice.(approx 20-25 grams)

Also, you can include a small portion of fruits and other treats 1-2 times a week. Please make sure you don't serve it regularly as it contains a lot of sugar in it.

Printed in Great Britain
by Amazon